THE FLOATING FIELD

How a Group of Thai Boys Built Their Own Soccer Field

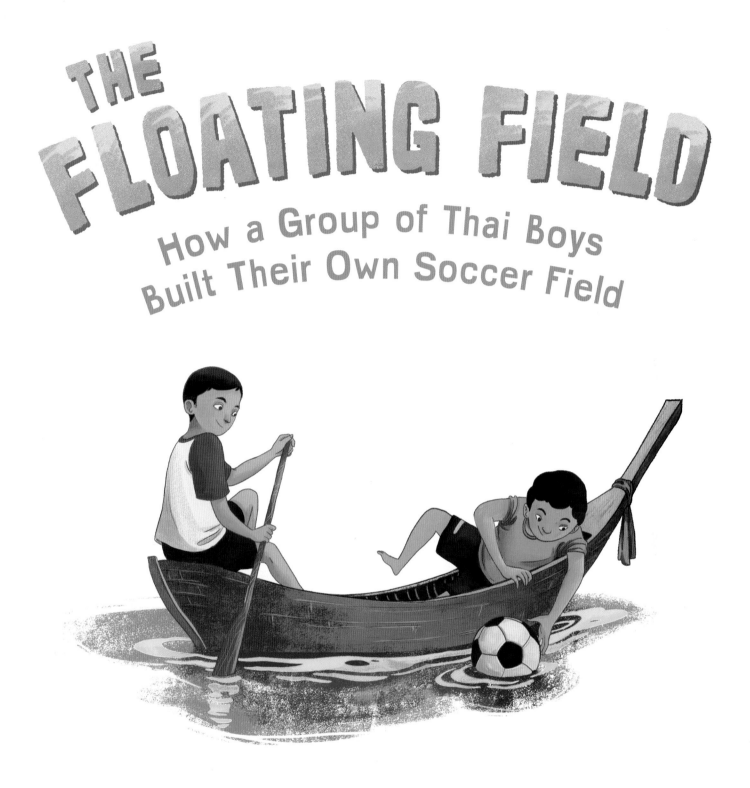

Scott Riley

Illustrated by **Nguyen Quang and Kim Lien**

Millbrook Press / Minneapolis

What's most important is that anything is possible. And as a community or team, you can overcome incredibly impossible odds.

—Prasit Hemmin, founding member of the Panyee Football Club

Prasit Hemmin lived in a village on stilts.

Prasit woke early each morning before school to help his father. Together, they loaded the longboat with nets while his mother brewed coffee and sliced jackfruit in the kitchen.

Like many villagers, Prasit's father spent his days fishing for groupers and prawns. He spent his nights tying nets and dreaming of the next day's catch.

But Prasit dreamed of things other than fish.
And last night, the moon had been full.

Prasit's father revved the boat's motor and headed out to sea. Prasit waved, then raced along the raised walkways to Uncle's coffee shop. The others were already there.

Uncle welcomed Prasit and his friends with plates of fried dough. Between sugary bites, the boys made important decisions. *Who will carry the poles? Who's on which team? Who gets to kick off first?*

Above them, the full moon had set and the sun was rising.
Below them, the tides were already shifting.

The moment school ended, the boys rushed to the pier. The tide was finally out, and a sandbar glistened in the distance. The boys jumped into a boat and paddled furiously.

Prasit and his friends planted the poles and got into position. With the ball in play, they dug in their toes and chased it across hard-packed ripples of sand. They weaved in between other players to get open.

And when they got close, they took a shot. **GOAL!**

Back and forth the boys played as longboats returned from the sea, full of fathers and fish. Waves soon crept in. The field narrowed. In minutes, the sandbar disappeared—and the game was over.

Prasit and his friends drifted back to the pier, their laughter echoing off the cliff. With the sandbar gone, the boys could only dream about playing until the tides were low enough once more.

watch the game they loved. The World Cup was on, and teams from across the globe were playing in a far-off place called Mexico. At Uncle's coffee shop, the boys huddled around the television— the only one on the island.

One day, after cheering for a team that came back from behind, someone suggested they form their own team. Everyone agreed.

But a real soccer team needed a real field.

Prasit looked out to where the sandbar lay hidden under the sea. He thought about their floating village built from nothing but wooden planks and metal roofs.

"We could make our own field," he offered. The boys nodded in agreement.

The next day after school, the boys scattered. Some searched for scraps of wood and empty barrels. Others swam out to abandoned fish farms to collect loose Styrofoam.

At the pier, they stacked materials and began building.
Hammers flew. Nails bent. Boards split.

Prasit and his friends had no plan. Somehow, that didn't matter.

For days, the boys collected wood
from broken boats and old docks.

Arms full, they hauled it all back to the pier.

Prasit handed planks down to boys in boats. Drifting in the tides, they fixed them to floating barrels and makeshift buoys.

Villagers heard what the boys were up to. Some walked by, shaking their heads. One even shouted, "You're crazy. Look around you. You can't play soccer—not here!"

But the boys didn't listen. Sea eagles wheeled overhead as they worked. Barrels and boards formed a platform. Some boys tethered it down below. Others painted the edges. A few began to frame knee-high goalposts.

After weeks of work, their floating field was complete. With fishnet goals at each end, it teetered in the waves.

No longer needing the moon to tug at the tides, Prasit and his friends headed straight to their field each day after school.

Loose boards and bent nails forced fancy footwork. So did the field's sidelines—when the ball bounced into the water, the kicker had to follow.

With the ball in play, they bounced on their toes and chased it across rickety boards. The ball moved faster now, and the boys raced to keep up.

They weaved in between other players to get
open. And when they got close, they took a shot.

GOAL!

Villagers still walked by, but they no longer shook their heads.
Instead, they stopped to watch. Some even cheered.

When news of an upcoming tournament on the mainland reached the island, the boys decided to take a chance and sign up.

On the morning of the tournament, Prasit and his friends walked to the pier in their mismatched jerseys and ragtag shorts.

Before their longboat pushed off, a group of villagers ran toward them. Some carried baskets. Others waved their hands.

The boys hadn't been the only ones planning for the tournament. Reaching into their baskets, friends and family members pulled out new jerseys, matching shorts, and a pair of cleats for each player. The boys beamed—so did the villagers.

The Panyee Football Club was born.

Later that morning on the mainland, the island boys got into position for their first game—this time on a field of grass.

Across from them, opponents bounced on toes, ready to play. Prasit and his team stood flat-footed, nervous.

But with the ball in play, the boys remembered what to do. They passed it down the field. They weaved in between other players to get open. And when they got close, they took a shot. GOAL!

By that afternoon, after winning several games, the Panyee Football Club had reached the semifinals.

Once again, Prasit and his team lined up and waited for the referee's whistle. As the game began, the sky darkened. Within minutes, sheets of rain came pouring down, drenching uniforms, filling cleats, and flooding the field.

The other team adjusted. Prasit's did not.

At the half, the Panyee Football Club was down 2–0.
The boys sat silently on the bench, raindrops pelting
their heads. They needed to turn the game around.

Prasit looked at his friends, his teammates.
He thought about how they played on their
floating field.

Reaching down, he unlaced his shoes and
peeled off his socks. His teammates
followed, nodding. Barefoot, they ran
back onto the field.

Without waterlogged shoes, the boys moved quickly, just like they always had. Passing give-and-gos and racing to the goal, the Panyee Football Club scored. Twice!

With only minutes to play, both teams battled for the ball. Finally, a player from the other team trapped it, dribbled down the field, and struck it one more time. The ball sailed into the net just past the goalie's reach.

The boys from Koh Panyee had lost.

But that day, in that very first tournament, the Panyee Football Club came in third place.

On their way back home, Prasit and his teammates yelled and cheered over the boat's rattling motor.

As the boys drifted back to the pier, their laughter echoed off the cliff once again. But this time, they didn't have to dream about when they'd play next. They had their floating field where they could play the game they loved, whenever they wanted.

AUTHOR'S NOTE

Soccer, known as *football* in many countries, is the world's most popular sport. In fact, more than 40 percent of the world's population consider themselves fans—that's almost half! These fans follow professional leagues each season, hoping that their team comes out on top. They also cheer on men's and women's national teams every four years in FIFA's World Cup Tournaments.

Koh Panyee's current floating field includes a blue covering and green plastic buoys.

If you're a fan, you probably know all this. You might also know that soccer is even more exciting to play than it is to watch. With a ball and a few friends, you can turn almost any space into a soccer field. That's exactly what players have done across the globe, sometimes in the most unexpected places—high atop a mountain in the Swiss Alps; in a village in the middle of the Amazon rain forest; on a building's rooftop in downtown Tokyo, Japan; and even on an ice shelf in the Arctic Circle.

Koh Panyee (KOH PAN-YEE) is one of those unexpected places. This fishing village, located on a tiny island off the coast of Thailand, is where Prasit Hemmin (PRAH-sit HEM-in) and his friends grew up loving soccer. Unfortunately for them, every inch of the village was taken for the school, houses, shops, and a mosque—there certainly wasn't room for a soccer field.

In this 2019 photo, the Panyee Football Club practices on a recently built paved platform next to the school.

The boys had to wait to play soccer on a sandbar that appeared during certain phases of the moon's cycle. Every day the moon's gravitational forces pull on the ocean, causing high and low tides. Twice a month—once when the moon is full and once when it is new—its alignment with the sun creates extra-strong spring tides. That was when the boys rushed to the sandbar soccer field to play.

In 2018, I first visited Koh Panyee and met Prasit. We sat at Uncle's coffee shop eating jackfruit and fried dough while he shared his story. He told me about his group of friends and how their love of soccer inspired them to build the floating field one board at a time. He shared stories about his experiences on the Panyee Football Club and how they eventually became regional champions in Thailand. And then he took me to the floating field. The original field is long gone, but the Thai government built the current floating field in honor of the boys and their team. I made a second visit to the island in 2019 to share my manuscript with Prasit, confirm details, and take additional photos—a few of which are included here.

Today, Prasit and his family still live on Koh Panyee. He says he is too old to play soccer, but he still roots for his favorite soccer teams including the Panyee Football Club he helped found. He now leads in other ways by developing a recycling program and working to reduce the cost of electricity on the island, which is six times greater than on the mainland. But Prasit doesn't work alone—he knows that when people work together, absolutely anything is possible.

Koh Panyee extends far into Phang Nga Bay. Its more recent walkways are made of logs and planks, while older walkways are made from concrete.

Koh Panyee's gold-domed mosque is a defining feature and cultural heart of the village.

PRASIT'S PERSPECTIVE

Hundreds of years ago, our ancestors chose to settle on this island for its calm waters and protected bay. Our fishing village existed quietly, almost neglected for generations. Tourists first began visiting after a famous James Bond movie was made on a nearby island in 1974, introducing the world to Phang Nga Bay and our village.

Football meant a lot to us kids on Koh Panyee in the 1980s. Especially for those of us who did not want to pursue the traditional way of fishing and living quietly, playing football allowed us to be active and dream big. We knew we were different growing up on an island, but if we played football, we thought we could connect with people on the mainland and gain their respect. We loved the game, and we really wanted to show we could play well even though we had no field.

My friends and I played on a sandbar near the mangrove forest during the spring tides every month. In 1986, we built the floating field. We kept playing to have fun and to prove to people outside that we could be good players. That year, we participated in the league tournament where we earned third place.

Years later, the Panyee Football Club won the provincial, regional, and national championships. My son was a player on that team. Now all of Thailand knows about Koh Panyee and its players. And so do you.

WORDS YOU MIGHT HEAR ON THE FLOATING FIELD

Pronunciation notes: Double vowels *aa*, *ii*, and *uu* are long vowel sounds. The *r* sound is rolled.

English	Thai	How to say it	Tips
ball	ลูกบอล	luuk-bawn	*uu* rhymes with *sue*
corner kick	เตะมุม	teh-moum	*moum* rhymes with *room*
dribble	เลี้ยงบอล	liang-bawn	
goal kick	ลูกเตะจากประตู	luuk-teh-jak-pratuu	*uu* rhymes with *sue*
goalkeeper	ผู้รักษาประตู	puu-raksa-pratuu	*uu* rhymes with *sue*
I'm open (spoken by a female)	ฉันว่าง ส่งมาๆ	chahn wahng sohng ma	
I'm open (spoken by a male)	ผมว่าง ส่งมาๆ	pohm wahng sohng ma	
kick, shoot	เตะ	teh	
nice save	รักษาประตูได้	raksa pratuu dai	*uu* rhymes with *sue*
offside	ล้ำหน้า	luhm-na	*luhm* rhymes with *hum*
pass	ส่ง	sohng	
player or athlete	นักกีฬา	nak-kii-laa	*kii* rhymes with *me* and *laa* rhymes with *ha*
shoot at the goal	ยิงประตู	ying pratuu	*uu* rhymes with *sue*
soccer	ฟุตบอล	fut-bawn	said almost like *football*
throw in	ทุ่ม	toum	said like the English word *tomb*
to make a goal	ทำประตู	tuhm pratuu	*tuhm* rhymes with *hum*

BIBLIOGRAPHY

Hemmin, Pasit. Interviews with the author, January 3, 2018; January 6, 2019.

Hutchinson, John. "Water Goal! Floating Football Pitch Surrounded by Azure Waters Opens in Thailand (Just Don't Kick the Ball Too Far!)." *Daily Mail* (London). Last modified November 28, 2014. https://www.dailymail.co.uk/travel/travel_news/article-2852625/Floating-football-pitch-keeps-Thai-tourist-blues-bay.html.

"Koh Panyi—The Floating, Fishing, Football Village." Thailand for Children. Accessed July 7, 2020. http://www.thailandforchildren.com/thailand-islands/phuket-family-holidays/koh-panyi-floating-fishing-football-village.

Suchontan, Cimi, et al. "Island Boys Beat Great Odds to Realize Football Dream." ThaiResidents.com, February 5, 2017. https://thairesidents.com/local/island-boys-beat-great-odds-realize-football-dream.

"A Tale of Passion." Vimeo video, 4:37. Posted by A World of Football. Accessed February 2, 2018. https://vimeo.com/41544315.

Taylor, Alan. "Photos: Soccer Fields around the World." *Atlantic*, June 14, 2018. https://www.theatlantic.com/photo/2018/06/photos-soccer-fields-around-the-world/562862/.

"World Football Report." Nielsen, December 6, 2018. https://www.nielsen.com/uk/en/insights/reports/2018/world-football-report.html.

FURTHER READING

Hoena, Blake. *Everything Soccer*. Washington, DC: National Geographic Children's Books, 2014.

Paul, Baptiste. *The Field*. Zurich: NorthSouth Books, 2018.

Puck. *Totally Epic, True & Wacky Soccer Facts & Stories*. Baltimore: duopress, 2017.

Raatma, Lucia. *It's Cool to Learn about Countries: Thailand*. Ann Arbor, MI: Cherry Lake, 2013.

Russell, Elaine. *All about Thailand: Stories, Songs, Crafts and Games for Kids*. Tokyo: Tuttle, 2016.

Taylor, Sean. *Goal!* New York: Henry Holt, 2014.

Thailand: *National Geographic Kids*
https://kids.nationalgeographic.com/explore/countries/thailand/

For Mom and Dad, who inspire me to dream beyond what
I think is possible
—S.R.

To our father and brothers, who love football so very much
—N.Q. and K.L.

Special thanks to Quincy Surasmith, Fon Chayanin Tanwongsval, and Wipaporn (Kate) Hongsopa for their assistance with the Thai soccer terms and pronunciations.

Millbrook Press™
An imprint of Lerner Publishing Group, Inc.
241 First Avenue North
Minneapolis, MN 55401 USA

For reading levels and more information, look up this title at www.lernerbooks.com.

Additional images on pp. 36–37: photos courtesy of the author; map by Laura Westlund/Independent Picture Service.

Designed by Viet Chu.
Main body text set in Imperfect OT bold. Typeface provided by T26.
The illustrations in this book were created with fineliner pen and Photoshop.

Library of Congress Cataloging-in-Publication Data

Names: Riley, Scott, 1970– author. | Quang, Nguyen, 1989– illustrator. | Lien, Kim, 1991–
    illustrator.
Title: The floating field : how a group of Thai boys built their own soccer field / Scott
    Riley ; illustrated by Nguyen Quang and Kim Lien.
Description: Minneapolis : Millbrook Press, [2021] | Includes bibliographical references. |
    Audience: Ages 7–11. | Audience: Grades 2–3. | Summary: "On a tiny Thai island without
    room for a soccer field, a group of resourceful teen boys gathers scraps and works
    together to build a floating field so they can play the game they love" —Provided by
    publisher.
Identifiers: LCCN 2020020857 (print) | LCCN 2020020858 (ebook) | ISBN 9781541579156
    (trade hardcover) | ISBN 9781728419008 (ebook)
Subjects: LCSH: Soccer—Thailand—Juvenile literature. | Soccer fields—Thailand—
    Juvenile literature. | Teamwork (Sports)—Juvenile literature.
Classification: LCC GV944.T5 R55 2021 (print) | LCC GV944.T5 (ebook) | DDC
    796.33409593—dc23

LC record available at https://lccn.loc.gov/2020020857
LC ebook record available at https://lccn.loc.gov/2020020858

Manufactured in China
4-52963-47901-3/7/2023